Did you know?

The world's largest sailing race is Bart's Bash. In 2014, the race involved 9,484 boats and took place in 237 different locations around the world.

Built for speed

How a boat is designed affects how safe it will be and how fast it will travel. The main part of a boat is called the hull. **Naval architects** use strong but lightweight materials, such as fibreglass and carbon fibre, to build the hulls of **powerboats** and **racing yachts**.

Moulds are used to get the shape needed for the hull.

Some yachts have more than one hull and are called multihull yachts. If a yacht has two hulls, it's called a **catamaran**. If it has three hulls, it's called a **trimaran**. Yachts with more than one hull are better for racing because they can reach much higher speeds!

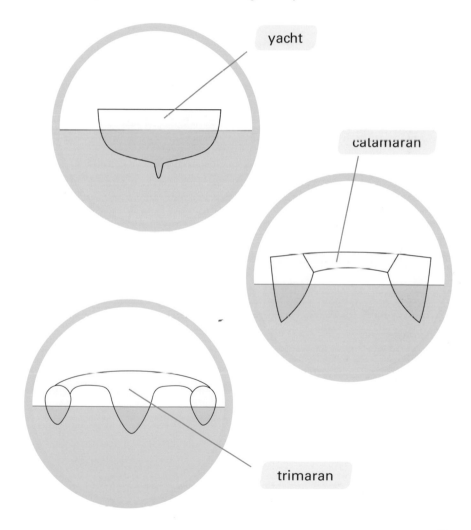

yacht

catamaran

trimaran

Yacht races

One of the most important yacht races is the America's Cup.
The competition is held between just two yachts.
Teams take part in other competitions throughout the year
to win points. The team with the most points gets to race
against the previous winners of the America's Cup.

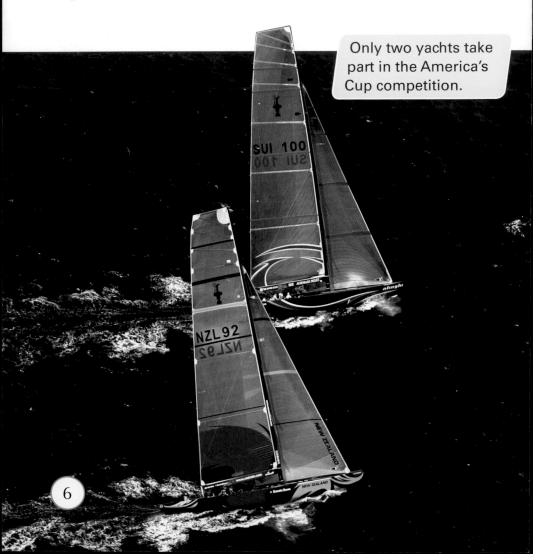

Only two yachts take part in the America's Cup competition.

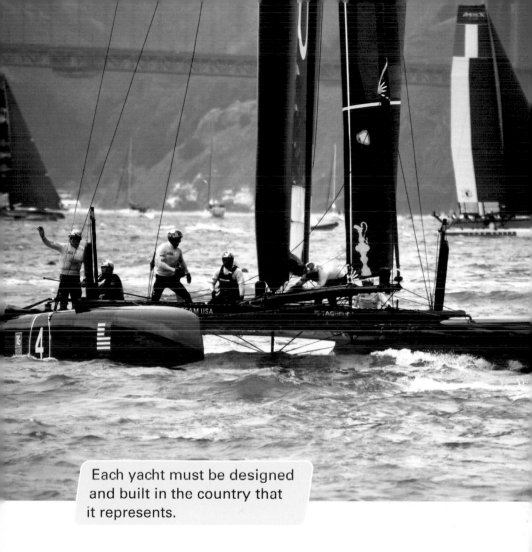

Each yacht must be designed and built in the country that it represents.

The previous winners of the America's Cup get to choose where the race will take place. This means they can choose somewhere that suits their team and boat.

The boats used in these races are very expensive to build. Teams use the latest technology in the hope they'll win.

Faster than the wind

Racing yachts can move faster than the wind!
Normal sailing boats use a cloth sail that fills with wind
and pushes the boat forward. But a racing yacht has a sail
that doesn't bend. This means that the wind hits the sail
hard and lifts the boat out of the water so it's almost flying.

Wings called **hydrofoils**
are attached to each hull of
this catamaran. They actually
lift the boat out of the water!

hydrofoil

Did you know?

The catamarans used in the America's Cup can reach speeds of up to 89 kilometres per hour!

Sailing around the world

The sport of sailing offers its competitors some tough challenges such as the Jules Verne Trophy for sailing around the world in the fastest time. Competitors face the trials of big seas, strong winds, storms, icebergs, cold and even snow to complete this race.

In 2000, Ellen MacArthur became the fastest woman to sail around the world on her own. In 2005, she became the fastest *person* to do this! She completed the voyage in 71 days, 14 hours and 18 minutes.

In 2008, Francis Joyon sailed around the world, on his own, in just 57 days!

In 2012, yachtsman Loïck Peyron and his team completed the round-the-world challenge in 45 days, 13 hours, 42 minutes and 53 seconds.

Powerful powerboats

Powerboats are designed for speed. They have a powerful engine at the back of the boat to drive them forward. Most powerboats have a wide, flat hull. This shape allows the boat to rise out of the water and helps it to travel faster.

This boat has a v-shaped **bow** that helps it to cut through the water at speed.

wide, flat hull

Some powerboats have two hulls. They have an engine
at the end of each hull and can reach speeds of over
200 kilometres per hour. At speeds like this,
the two-person crew needs to wear
fireproof suits and helmets
in case they crash.

engine

a twin-hull powerboat

v-shaped bow

The power to go

Racing powerboats have their engines permanently built into their hulls, but other types of motorboats may have an **outboard motor** that can be removed.

Inboard motors work like car engines. They use fuel to drive a motor, which powers the propellers and makes them spin. The faster the motor goes, the faster the propellers spin and the faster the boat travels.

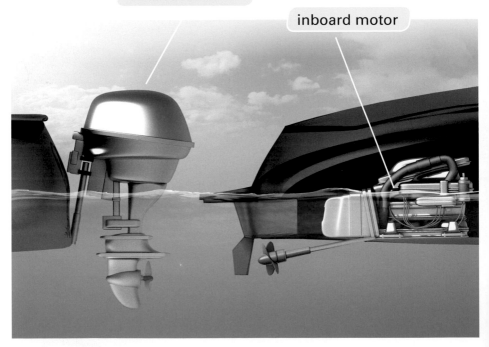

outboard motor

inboard motor

Some boats have motors that power a **jet drive**. The jet drive sucks up water and then forces the water out at the back of the boat, which pushes the boat forward.

Did you know?

An engine can get very hot so it needs to be cooled by water. Boats pump water from outside to cool their engines.

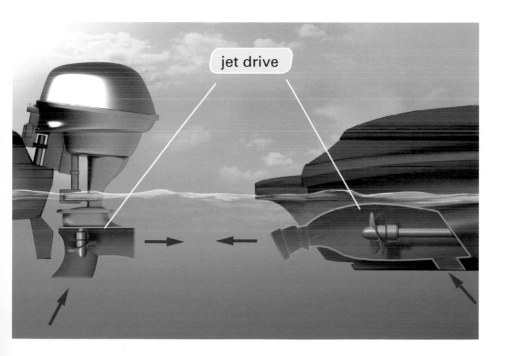

jet drive

Powerboat races

There are different types of powerboat races. Some races are called circuit races and take place on lakes or rivers. Boats reach speeds of about 200 kilometres per hour in some circuit races. Other races are held on the sea and are called offshore races.

Endurance racing is where competitors race to complete a set route – around Britain, for example, or even around the world!

The driver of a **hydroplane** either sits, kneels or lies down to race it!

Competitors in the World Powerboat Championship often reach speeds of over 200 kilometres per hour.

The World Powerboat Championship is famous for being the roughest, toughest ocean race in the world. Teams from all over the world compete in this offshore race which is considered one of the most amazing motorsports in the world. It's the Formula 1 of boat racing!

Power record-breakers

Donald Campbell had already set the water speed record seven times, but he wanted the challenge of breaking it again. So in 1964, he travelled to Lake Dumbleyung in Western Australia with his **jet-powered boat**, *Bluebird K7*. Campbell's *Bluebird K7* reached a record-breaking speed of 444.71 kilometres per hour.

Did you know?

Donald Campbell is the only person ever to have set both the land and water speed record in the same year.

By 1967, *Bluebird K7* had a new engine and Donald Campbell was set to try again. He travelled to Lake Coniston, England for another attempt. Sadly, *Bluebird K7* flipped at high speed and Campbell was killed in the attempt.

Bluebird K7 had engine problems during testing on Lake Coniston.

Spirit of Australia

In 1978, Campbell's water speed record was broken by Ken Warby. He reached speeds of 511.11 kilometres per hour in his boat, *Spirit of Australia*. **Mechanical engineer** Warby designed *Spirit of Australia* at his kitchen table and built it in his back garden.

Warby's record still stands today. However, Warby is working with his son to build *Spirit of Australia II*.

Did you know?

In 2008, *Earthrace* became the world's first powerboat to travel around the world using only **renewable** fuels. It's also the first boat to be built using plant fibres.

Super yachts

Super yachts are luxury boats. Owners often want to have the most fabulous boat possible, so many super yachts have on-board swimming pools, cinemas and even helicopter pads!

Super yacht owners will **redesign** existing boats to make them bigger and better.

One of the most impressive super yachts is called *Motor Yacht A*. It's 119 metres long and has three swimming pools! The glass floor to one of the swimming pools also forms the ceiling to the disco below.

Motor Yacht A has been designed to look like it has an upside-down hull.

Super record-breakers

Owners can be very competitive when it comes to the size of their yachts. Larry Ellison ordered his yacht, *Rising Sun*, to be 120 metres long. But when he found out that someone else had ordered a yacht that would be 127 metres long, Ellison extended his yacht to be 138 metres long!

Rising Sun has a basketball court that can also be used as a helicopter pad.

Rising Sun is still not as big as *Azzam,* which was built in 2013 for the **emir** of Abu Dhabi. *Azzam* is 180 metres long and is the world's largest yacht.

The owner of *Azzam* wanted the yacht to be luxurious, while also being able to travel at high speed.

Boat shows

Boat shows are held around the world to promote new products and businesses. Visitors can explore the latest boating technologies and gadgets. Exciting new boat designs are also shown off at these international events.

The Dubai Boat Show

The world's largest solar boat is powered by 809 panels.

The Dubai Boat Show is an important event in the boating world. It's held over five days and attracts over 28,000 visitors from around the world. Visitors can see a wide variety of equipment and boats for sailing, fishing, diving, water sports, or just for luxury. They can experience the power of the boats for themselves by taking part in some of the demonstrations.

Glossary

bow	front of a boat
catamaran	boat with two hulls
emir	commander, general or prince
hydrofoils	wings attached to the bottom of a boat
hydroplane	a light motorboat that skims the water with only the back part of the hull touching the water
inboard motors	engines built into a boat
jet drive	part of a boat's engine that forces out water to push the boat forward
jet-powered boat	boat with an engine that uses a jet drive
mechanical engineer	person who designs machines
moulds	hollow forms, used to create particular shapes
naval architects	people who design boats
outboard motor	motor that can be removed from a boat
powerboats	boats with an engine designed for travelling fast
racing yachts	boats with rigid sails that are designed for racing
redesign	changing the way something looks
renewable	something that can be used again
trimaran	boat with three hulls

Index

Size and speed

Family car

4.5 metres

Motor Yacht A

119 metres

Rising Sun

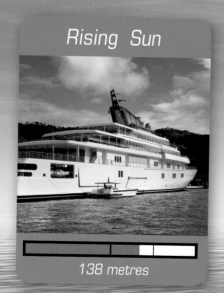

138 metres

Azzam

180 metres

Family car

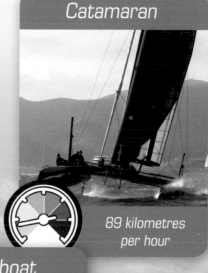

50 kilometres per hour

Catamaran

89 kilometres per hour

Powerboat

200 kilometres per hour

Bluebird K7

445 kilometres per hour

Spirit of Australia

511 kilometres per hour

Ideas for reading

Written by Clare Dowdall, PhD
Lecturer and Primary Literacy Consultant

Reading objectives:
- retrieve and record information from non-fiction
- read for a range of purposes
- discuss their understanding and explain the meaning of words in context

Spoken language objectives:
- give well-structured descriptions, explanations and narratives for different purposes

Curriculum links: Design and technology: design and make

Resources: paper and pencils, materials for building paper boats and testing their buoyancy, ICT for research

Build a context for reading

- Look at the front cover. Ask children to make a list of what super boats can do.
- Read the blurb together. Discuss children's experiences of being on different types of boats. Challenge children to use their senses to support descriptions.
- Ask children to skim the contents and identify as many different types of boats as possible that feature.

Understand and apply reading strategies

- Read pp2–3 together. Model how to retrieve information from the text by skimming for information about different types of boats and the jobs that they do. Use your finger to skim quickly for specific information.
- Help children to use the images to support their comprehension. Challenge them to look carefully and apply their observations about the boats to the written text, e.g. discuss what the cruise ship does and contains.